KEVIN ELYOT

Playwright and actor Kevin Elyot was born in Birmingham and educated at King Edward's School and Bristol University.

As well as *The Day I Stood Still,* his stage plays include *Coming Clean* (1982), for which he won the Samuel Beckett Award, *Consent* (1989), *The Moonstone* (1990), adapted from Wilkie Collins, a new translation of Ostrovsky's *Artists and Admirers* (1992), and *My Night with Reg* (1994), which won both the Evening Standard and Laurence Olivier Awards for Best Comedy, as well as Writers' Guild and Critics' Circle Awards. His screenplays include *Killing Time* (BBC, 1990), which won the Writers' Guild Award, a two-part adaptation of *The Moonstone* (BBC, 1996) and the film version of *My Night with Reg* (BBC Films, 1997). He has also written for radio.

A Selection of Other Volumes in this Series

Simon Block
CHIMPS
NOT A GAME FOR BOYS

Jez Butterworth
MOJO

Jean Cocteau
LES PARENTS TERRIBLES

Kevin Elyot
MY NIGHT WITH REG

William Gaminara
ACCORDING TO HOYLE

Pam Gems
DEBORAH'S DAUGHTER
STANLEY

Godfrey Hamilton
ROAD MOVIE

Robert Holman
BAD WEATHER

Stephen Jeffreys
THE CLINK
A GOING CONCERN
THE LIBERTINE

Ayub Khan-Din
EAST IS EAST

Larry Kramer
THE DESTINY OF ME
THE NORMAL HEART

Tony Kushner
ANGELS IN AMERICA:
    Parts One and Two
A BRIGHT ROOM
    CALLED DAY
SLAVS!

Mike Leigh
ECSTASY
SMELLING A RAT

Conor McPherson
ST NICHOLAS & THE WEIR
THIS LIME TREE BOWER

Terence Rattigan
AFTER THE DANCE
THE BROWNING VERSION
FRENCH WITHOUT TEARS
THE WINSLOW BOY

Billy Roche
THE CAVALCADERS
POOR BEAST IN THE RAIN
THE WEXFORD TRILOGY

Michel Tremblay
THE GUID SISTERS

Nicholas Wright
MRS KLEIN

Kevin Elyot

THE DAY
I STOOD STILL

NICK HERN BOOKS
London

A Nick Hern Book

The Day I Stood Still first published in Great Britain
as a paperback original in 1998 by Nick Hern Books Ltd,
14 Larden Road, London W3 7ST

The Day I Stood Still copyright © 1998 by Kevin Elyot

Kevin Elyot has asserted his moral right to be identified as
the author of this work

Front cover photo: copyright David Whyte

Extracts from the song 'To Love Somebody'
by Barry and Robin Gibb reprinted with permission

Typeset by Country Setting, Woodchurch, Kent TN26 3TB
Printed by Cox and Wyman Ltd, Reading Berks

A CIP catalogue record for this book is available from
the British Library

ISBN 1 85459 334 X

And still I return like a line to the centre,
Like fire to the sun and the stream to the sea.

Monteverdi, *L'Incoronazione di Poppea*
Act 1, Scene i. Libretto: Busenello

The Day I Stood Still was first performed in the Cottesloe
auditorium of the Royal National Theatre on 22 January 1998.
The cast was as follows:

HORACE	Adrian Scarborough/Callum Dixon
JUDY	Catherine Russell/Daisy Beaumont
GUY	Geoffrey Church
TERENCE	Jake Wood/Joseph Swash
JIMI/JERRY	Oliver Milburn

Musicians Bernie Lafontaine (clarinets), Graeme Taylor
(guitar)

Director   Ian Rickson
Designer   Mark Thompson
Lighting   Hugh Vanstone
Music   Stephen Warbeck
Dialect Coach   Joan Washington
Company Voice Work   Patsy Rodenburg
Movement   Jane Gibson
Sound   Simon Baker

Characters

HORACE

JUDY

GUY

TERENCE

JIMI

JERRY

Location

The sitting-room of an upper-storey apartment in a North
London mansion block. There is a small balcony with a railing
and outside shutters. The furniture includes a late Georgian
dining-chair and a Victorian upright piano.

Casting

Horace, Judy and Terence should each be played by two actors.
Jimi and Jerry should be played by one actor.

SCENE ONE

Early evening. JUDY *is embracing* HORACE. HORACE
wears glasses. GUY *looks on with a carrier-bag.* JUDY *breaks
the embrace.*

HORACE. The thing is –

JUDY. Have you lost weight?

HORACE. Ye-

 She embraces him again.

JUDY. It's so gorgeous to see you. Just gorgeous.

GUY. Gorgeous.

 She breaks the embrace.

HORACE. You must be Guy.

GUY (*French*). Guy.

JUDY. Clarified butter, not Bonfire Night.

GUY. Enchanté, Horace.

HORACE (*extending a hand*). Pleased to meet you –

 GUY *ignores the hand and kisses him twice.*

JUDY. Oh, Horry!

HORACE. I'm completely lost for words.

JUDY. Is this a bad time? .

HORACE. No, no. It's just that –

JUDY. We got in yesterday, we're off again tomorrow, and I
 thought I must see Horace. So here we are!

HORACE. Here we are, indeed! Gosh! I haven't got a thing in,
 I'm afraid.

JUDY. We can't stop.

HORACE. Just some Ryvita and . . . you see, the thing is –

JUDY. I hope you don't mind, but Guy's brought a little snack.

GUY. A little snack.

HORACE. Has he?

JUDY. And something lovely to wash it down with. Instant celebration!

HORACE. That's very kind of you, but Judy –

JUDY. Do you mind if I give the nanny a quick call?

HORACE. Of course not. Help yourself.

JUDY. Only she's new, and Puerto Rican. (*Dialling.*) It's so gorgeous to see you.

HORACE. How is Jimi?

GUY. The kitchen is . . . ?

HORACE. Oh, yes. It's . . .

He leads GUY *out, surreptitiously checking his watch.*

JUDY (*on the phone*). Elvira, how is he? . . . Where is he? . . . What's he doing? . . . Well, make sure he doesn't sit on it . . . We won't be long.

She replaces the receiver as HORACE *comes back in.*

We took her on just before we left. Guy's rather fond of her. I'm not so sure. Apparently, she's worked for the Claptons.

HORACE. He says he's okay in there, but I feel a bit –

JUDY. Oh, he'll be fine. He's happiest in a kitchen.

HORACE. If you're sure.

JUDY. I'm sure.

HORACE. It's just rather odd having –

JUDY. You don't mind?

HORACE. No. I hope he doesn't. It's a bit of a mess, actually.

JUDY. Don't worry. He'll be fine.

HORACE. Good. So Jimi's alright, is he?

JUDY. Oh, adorable.

HORACE. It'd be nice to see him.

JUDY. I know, I know. Maybe on our way back.

HORACE. Only I'd like to make a good fist of being a godparent rather than just –

JUDY. Of course, yes, and I want that too. It's just so tight this time, but as I say, coming back, maybe there'll be –

HORACE. I was so touched – that I was asked.

JUDY. You look really well.

HORACE. Judy, the thing is –

Enter GUY.

GUY. Oil?

HORACE. Pardon?

GUY. Oil.

HORACE. Oil. Oh, yes. On the window-sill.

GUY. Window . . . ?

JUDY. Le rebord.

GUY. Ah, bon.

He's gone.

HORACE. Why does he want oil?

JUDY. For the mayonnaise.

HORACE. Mayonnaise!

JUDY. For the asparagus.

HORACE. I thought it was a snack.

JUDY. It is a snack. He's unbelievable.

HORACE. He must be. Mayonnaise is quite hard, isn't it?

JUDY. He saw this asparagus and just couldn't resist it. That little greengrocer down the road . . .

HORACE. Oh, yes.

JUDY. There's something about him, isn't there?

HORACE. The greengrocer?

JUDY. Guy.

HORACE. Oh, (*English.*) Guy . . . (*French.*) Guy. Yes, he seems nice.

JUDY. My first taste of the older man. He's not exactly Belmondo, but he makes up for it in other ways. He's an angel. An angel. I didn't know what the hell to do – should I stay, come back? I hadn't a clue. Then Guy appeared and everything fell into place.

HORACE. So you'll be staying there?

JUDY. Oh, yes. I'm moving into his apartment. It's a much better location than – where I am now. It's the block next to Woody Allen's.

HORACE. Really?

JUDY. He's got a cow on the roof – Woody Allen, that is – it's not real – and Lilian Gish is on the other side.

HORACE. Well!

JUDY. You must come and visit.

HORACE. I've never been.

JUDY. Oh, you absolutely must.

HORACE. Maybe I will.

JUDY. It's the best place in the world.

HORACE. I'm not that keen on travel, you know. I like watching travel programmes and I find that kind of enough. Going's always a let-down, don't you think?

JUDY. God, I couldn't survive without travelling.

HORACE. It's a real shock to see you.

JUDY. A shock?

HORACE. A nice shock. But when I opened the door –

JUDY. I couldn't resist dropping in. You don't mind?

HORACE. No, only when I opened the door, I thought –

JUDY. God, this is strange.

HORACE. Is it?

JUDY. Being here.

HORACE. Yes. I'm thinking of doing something with it. I still see mum and dad everywhere.

JUDY. Like what?

HORACE. What?

JUDY. What were you thinking of doing with it?

HORACE. I don't know. Maybe making the balcony bigger.

JUDY. How would you do that?

HORACE. I don't know. Or knocking a wall down or something. It's nice, though, isn't it?

JUDY. You'll take root.

HORACE. It's not that long.

JUDY. I've lost count of the places I've lived. You should move.

HORACE. It's nice.

JUDY. Don't you feel it's time?

HORACE. No.

Enter GUY.

GUY. Do you have a . . . ?

He does a mime.

HORACE. Pepper-mill?

The mime continues.

Screwdriver?

GUY (*still miming*). For the . . . ?

JUDY. Qu'est-ce que tu veux, dindon?

GUY. Un pilon et mortier.

JUDY. Pestle and mortar.

HORACE. Sorry.

GUY. Okay.

He's gone.

HORACE. A pestle and mortar? Why does he want that?

JUDY. I don't know. Garlic, herbs . . .

HORACE. For what?

JUDY. He's such a sweetheart. He just doesn't get English
at all.

HORACE. How does he get by?

JUDY. Fine, fine.

HORACE. But doesn't he need to understand what people are
talking about as a psychotherapist?

JUDY. Oh, but he does understand. He does. Language isn't
everything, Horace.

HORACE. Right.

JUDY. And lots of his clients don't speak English anyway.
What are you doing at the moment?

HORACE. I'm still at the museum.

JUDY. Still?

HORACE. Yes.

JUDY. You'll ossify if you're not careful.

HORACE. I like my job. When I don't, I'll change.

JUDY. But you're in your prime. Any minute now, you'll start
slipping into middle age.

HORACE. Not yet.

JUDY. Not long. You should be doing things and going places.

HORACE. I don't want to. I'm fine as I am. I like this place, and I've got my music, my books, a friend or two. Honestly, Jude, I'm okay. I'm fairly happy.

JUDY. Do you still write?

HORACE. Well, you know . . . Judy, the thing is –

JUDY. What?

HORACE. Someone's coming.

JUDY. We're not stopping.

HORACE. No, but he might be here (*Checking watch.*) fairly soon.

JUDY. Would that be a problem?

HORACE. No, but I thought I ought to warn you. In fact, I'll just . . .

HORACE *goes to the balcony and looks down.* JUDY *notices the piano. He re-enters.*

I'm sorry, would you like a drink or something?

JUDY. We can go, if you'd prefer.

HORACE. Honestly, that's not what I mean. I just thought I ought to – let you know. That's all.

JUDY. Dear old Horry! I don't think I've ever seen you slimmer.

HORACE. I wouldn't say slim.

JUDY. Comparatively.

HORACE. There's still a way to go.

JUDY. Did you ever try getting your novel published again?

HORACE. You give up after a while. I thought I should try another one, something new.

JUDY. Good.

HORACE. Yes.

JUDY. And are you?

HORACE. Yes. Well . . . you know. I sometimes wonder how
many ideas a person has in a lifetime – good ones, that is.
One or two, if you're lucky.

JUDY. I'd have thought a few more than that.

HORACE. I mean, most of us don't have anything to say, do
we, that really needs saying, or anything to do that's that
important, and most of the time we're thinking about
nothing in particular, aren't we?

JUDY. I've never had time to think about it.

HORACE. Maybe it's just me.

JUDY. What if you've already had the couple of ideas you're
going to have in your life?

HORACE. Now there's a thought.

Enter GUY *with three glasses of wine, which he passes
round.*

GUY. In ten minutes, we have a gorgeous snack.

JUDY. You darling! Horry, I can't tell you how lucky I am!
He's so good at it.

GUY. Ma petite figue –

JUDY. And he can cook. (*Toasting.*) À la vôtre!

GUY. À la vôtre!

HORACE. À la – cheers . . .

They drink.

GUY. You like chocolate?

HORACE. Yes. Yes, I do, actually.

GUY. Because in the kitchen I find a drawer full of Mars bars.

HORACE. Ah –

JUDY. Horry!

HORACE. They were on special offer.

JUDY (*to* GUY). You shouldn't be going through people's drawers.

He embraces her.

Well, maybe some people's . . . Dindon . . .

He fondles her.

Ooh, dindon . . . (*Gently breaking the embrace.*) Non. So have you got anyone?

HORACE. In what sense?

JUDY. You know exactly what I mean. (*To* GUY.) He's always been a bit of a dark horse, even as a boy.

GUY. A black stallion.

JUDY. Yes, I didn't quite mean that.

GUY *wanders on to the balcony.*

HORACE. That was practically the last time you saw me.

JUDY. When?

HORACE. As a boy.

JUDY. Nonsense. We've met loads of times since then.

HORACE. Not loads, Jude. A handful, maybe.

JUDY. It's hard keeping up. Time vanishes, doesn't it?

HORACE. I know. It just happens like that. I know.

JUDY. So have you?

HORACE. Pardon?

JUDY. Met anyone.

HORACE. Well, to tell you the truth, the someone I'm expecting is –

JUDY. Horry!

HORACE. Yes. That's why it's all a bit –

JUDY. How long have you been seeing him?

HORACE. Oh, er –

JUDY. You little bugger! I can't wait! We can all have nibbles together.

HORACE. Judy –

JUDY. And then we'll leave you to it, don't worry!

GUY. The view is fantastic.

HORACE. When it's clear, you can see the Downs.

GUY. Ah, the Downs!

HORACE. Yes.

GUY. What are the Downs?

HORACE. Sort of hills.

JUDY. Collines.

GUY. Ah! Les collines!

HORACE. Yes.

GUY. A beautiful apartment.

HORACE. Thank you. There are one or two little drawbacks, but –

GUY. Drawbacks?

HORACE. Problems.

GUY. Ah, oui.

HORACE. Well, one problem, really –

A church clock starts to strike the hour. Its proximity makes it alarmingly loud.

JUDY. Jesus Christ!

HORACE (*checking his watch*). It'll be –

Stroke two.

– over soon.

JUDY. How the hell – ?

Stroke three.

How the hell do you live with that?

Stroke four.

HORACE. It's a case of having to, really. You kind of –

Stroke five.

Anyway, you've heard it before.

JUDY. Have I?

Stroke six.

It was never that loud, surely.

HORACE. It's never changed.

Stroke seven. Silence.

GUY. So.

HORACE. So.

GUY. So what is the problem?

HORACE. That was it.

GUY. Ah, bon.

JUDY (*indicating hallway*). Darling . . . I can't quite remember –

HORACE. It's at the end of the passage.

JUDY. Bless you.

She exits.

GUY. There's someone down there.

HORACE *darts on to the balcony.*

HORACE. Where?

GUY. Oh! Disparu!

HORACE. Where did he go?

GUY. Je ne sais pas.

HORACE. Was he just standing there?

GUY. He look up and then – disparu.

HORACE. Oh.

GUY. Perhaps he go into the trees.

HORACE. Yes. Anyway . . .

GUY. She is so beautiful.

HORACE. Judy?

GUY. So beautiful and good.

HORACE. Mm.

GUY. Me, I am surprised, the age I am, that she would join with me.

HORACE. You're not very old. And she seems happy enough.

GUY. I hope. You, she like very much.

HORACE. Does she? We hardly see each other.

GUY. You are old friends.

HORACE. In that we met a long time ago, yes. She sort of pops into my life now and again.

GUY. But you are a godparent?

HORACE. Yes, although I rather think that might have had more to do with Jerry. Did you meet him?

GUY. No, unfortunately.

HORACE. He was another old friend I hardly ever saw. In fact, I didn't hear that he'd died until after the funeral. I suppose Judy had so much on her plate and, apparently, it was all very low-key.

GUY. Do you want kids?

HORACE. No. No, I don't think so.

GUY. You don't like them?

HORACE. From when they're about fifteen I do. No, no, I didn't mean that. Yes, I like kids. Sort of. I'd like to see more of Jimi. I've only met him the once, at the christening. They came over here for that, what with family and things. I was really touched when I was asked to be a godfather. It came completely out of the blue. I mean, we hadn't been in contact for ages. I'd like to see Jimi grow up and do whatever children do, but as you live in New York – well, I won't get the chance, I suppose. C'est la vie!

GUY. Ah, oui. C'est vrai.

HORACE. Oui.

They drink.

GUY. I hate New York.

HORACE. Do you?

GUY. A terrible place, and for children . . . You know something, Harris –

HORACE. Horace.

GUY. I want to live again in France – and Jimi, so beautiful for him. Don't say nothing, but I hope that Judy, when she see my family and the place we live, I hope she think, 'Ah, yes, I would love to live here!'

HORACE. Mm. She's quite strong-willed, though, isn't she? And what with her career –

GUY. But la France – paradis! You know it?

HORACE. When I was a boy, I went to Calais to stay with a penfriend, but we didn't really hit it off.

GUY. You must go back.

HORACE. To Calais?

GUY. To France.

HORACE. Yes, maybe. Perhaps.

GUY. You understand me?

HORACE. Yes: you think I should go back to France.

GUY. No, no – my accent, is it very strong?

HORACE. Well, it's – there, but then again, you're French.

GUY. But you understand what I say?

HORACE. Oh, yes. We've all got accents, I suppose.

GUY. You have an accent?

HORACE. I've probably got a bit of something or other, and Judy used to have an accent, apparently, when she was a girl.

GUY. Judy?

HORACE. Yes. She comes from Birmingham originally. Now, that's a very strange accent.

GUY. She still has it?

HORACE. No. She'd lost it by the time I met her. But I remember that, if you took her unawares, like waking her up or something, she'd lurch into Brummie without thinking about it and then get very cross.

GUY. Brummie?

Enter JUDY.

JUDY. Are you telling him all my secrets?

HORACE. I don't know your secrets.

JUDY (*embracing him*). Oh, Guy, Guy!

They kiss.

Do you know, Horace, when he combs his hair, he can make sparks fly?

HORACE. Gosh.

JUDY. You can actually hear it crackle.

GUY. Mes cheveux, oui. Electric.

HORACE. Gosh.

JUDY. I think you should check les asperges. They're getting a bit jumpy.

GUY. Ah, bon.

He exits.

JUDY. Could I just give Elvira a quick tinkle?

HORACE. Yes, yes.

JUDY (*dialling*). The poor baby won't know which continent
he's on . . . Elvira, how is he? . . . Let me speak to him . . .
Jimjams, sweetie! . . . It's mummy, silly . . . Are you being a
good Jimjams? . . . You darling sweetie heart! . . . (*Handing
him the phone.*) Say hello.

HORACE. What?

JUDY. Speak to him.

HORACE. What should I say?

JUDY. Anything you like. He's four; he can talk.

HORACE. Jimi . . . Jimi . . .

JUDY. What's he say?

HORACE. He's breathing heavily.

JUDY. The flight's left him blocked.

HORACE. Jimi . . . (*Taking phone from ear.*) Ow!

JUDY. What?

HORACE. He blew a raspberry.

JUDY. Funny little thing! (*Into the phone.*) Funny little darling,
aren't you? (*To* HORACE.) Carry on. He'll probably
recognise your voice.

HORACE. Judy, the only time we've met, he was being
dangled over a font. We've hardly bonded.

JUDY. Say something.

HORACE. Jimi . . . It's Horace . . .

Beat.

JUDY. What's he say?

HORACE. Nothing . . . Jimi! Hello! (*To* JUDY.) He said hello.

JUDY. Ah!

HORACE. Yes? . . . Yes . . .

JUDY. What did he say?

HORACE. He said, would I give him a shiny new pound.

JUDY. Oh, the darling darling! (*Taking the phone.*) My little treasure, of course Horrid Horace will give you a shiny new pound . . . Now you be a good boy . . . Bye bye, my darling . . . bye bye, darling . . . bye bye . . . bye . . .

She puts down the phone.

Ohh! He said, (*Imitating* JIMI.) 'The fairy come to see me.'

HORACE. The fairy?

JUDY. Yes, the honey. He thinks a fairy watches over him at night. Isn't that sweet? He does make me laugh. He's just getting into the pooh-willy-bum phase. Mind you, that can get a little tiresome.

HORACE. How long does that last?

JUDY. From the men I know, the rest of his life. Oh God, I do hope not! When I see him playing with his willy and other boys' willies, I wonder will he ever take silk or do something clever in the City.

HORACE. Or follow in his father's footsteps.

JUDY. He's not musical.

HORACE. He's four.

JUDY. I do adore him so.

HORACE. What do I actually do as a godparent?

JUDY. I'm not sure.

HORACE. I mean, if you dropped down dead, would one of us take over? Isn't that the sort of thing a godparent does?

JUDY. I've already made arrangements for that eventuality.

HORACE. Oh.

JUDY. Flossie and Caulfield would take him in.

HORACE. Flossie and who?

JUDY. Caulfield, Flossie's other half. She's my best mate. They live in The Dakota. Fabulous apartment.

HORACE. But what if they died?

JUDY. Well, I don't know. I suppose my mother would look after him.

HORACE. And what if she died?

JUDY. It'd be fucking bad luck!

HORACE. I was just wondering.

JUDY. Dying's not part of my game-plan.

HORACE. Does Jimi still have that (*Touching his forehead.*) – ?

JUDY. No, he doesn't.

HORACE. Oh. Did you – ?

JUDY. It went.

HORACE. Oh.

> GUY *comes into the room with the open bottle of wine and tops everyone up.*

So where are you actually en route to?

GUY. En route! Ah, oui!

JUDY. He's taking us to meet la famille, aren't you, my love?

GUY. Ah, ma famille, ma famille . . .

JUDY. They're just above the Camargue, a tiny village called Vieille-

GUY. Vergervieux.

JUDY. Vergervieux, that's it, and apparently they have a fantastic house called Le Chardonneret. Lovely name, isn't it?

GUY. Beautiful in pie.

HORACE. Isn't it a wine?

JUDY. A finch, darling.

GUY. A bird.

JUDY. That's what I said.

GUY. Very beautiful.

JUDY. A goldfinch, I think. Fabulous colours.

GUY. En croute. (*He kisses his fingers.*)

JUDY. Guy, darling, you can't eat them.

GUY. Tourte au chardonneret – fantastic!

JUDY. They're pretty little fluffy things. You wouldn't want
    to put one in your mouth.

GUY. Fluffy?

JUDY. And they've also got use of a pool which they share
    with a couple of gites.

GUY. I cook for you.

JUDY. No, dindon, pas de chardonneret, jamais!

GUY. Judy –

JUDY. Okay?

GUY. Okay.

   Beat.

HORACE. I wouldn't know one bird from another.

GUY. I get the snack.

   He goes out.

HORACE. I just need to check . . .

   He goes on to the balcony and looks down. JUDY *looks at
   the piano, then touches it.* HORACE *comes back in.*

JUDY. Is this the one . . . ?

HORACE. The one that Jerry played, yes.

JUDY. It was so long ago.

HORACE. Some things stay in your mind.

JUDY. Yes.

HORACE. It was a nice time.

JUDY. I can only remember bits. I know I'm rather naughty about keeping in touch.

HORACE. It takes two. And you've got a lot on.

JUDY. Well, yes. I simply can't afford to slouch.

HORACE. I'm sure you can't.

JUDY. You know I'm associate editor now.

HORACE. No. That's great, Jude.

JUDY. Yes. It was so strange how we . . . how Jerry and I kept coming back together. Little asteroids colliding. Just when I thought, well, that's it, that's over, we'd meet by chance, or really like it was always meant to be, and when I had Jimi and we finally tried living together like people do . . . He wasn't easy, Horace. I know you had a soft spot for him, but . . . when you actually live with someone . . . It wasn't easy. What a waste! He was the most gifted person. He could have been a great pianist.

HORACE. Yes.

JUDY. A great pianist. Lots of people think this. But he wouldn't play the game. He had it all and, for some God-forsaken reason, he didn't want to know. And now: nothing! It makes me so fucking angry.

HORACE. Yes, but if he didn't want to –

JUDY. If you have the gifts, it's your duty to use them. Otherwise, what the hell's the point?

She produces a cigarette case and takes out a small joint.

Do you mind?

HORACE. No.

JUDY. A relaxant from Hawaii.

She lights it and inhales loudly and deeply. She passes it to HORACE, *who inspects it.*

There's this woman, she hangs round our neighbourhood, a sort of bag-lady, and she thinks she's in a queue. She takes a step forward, then stops, and waits, then she takes another step and waits again. Darling, it doesn't do anything for you if you just look at it.

HORACE. Sorry.

He takes a small puff.

JUDY. I can't bear to see her. She makes me want to scream.

She takes the joint from HORACE *and proceeds to smoke it voraciously as she speaks, down to the last millimetres.*

I keep hoping she'll drop down dead or get run over – but no. When we left for the airport yesterday, she was outside our apartment block, still in her queue.

HORACE. She's probably English.

JUDY. Jerry was drinking like a fish. Did you know that?

HORACE. How would I?

JUDY. And God knows what else he was on!

HORACE. He was always a bit of a rebel.

JUDY. Most people grow out of it.

HORACE. Well, maybe.

JUDY. He didn't understand me. I'm not sure he wanted to. I wonder if two people can ever understand each other, their deepest feelings and thoughts? Physically, we were – well, obscenely intimate, but we remained apart. The more intimate we were, the more isolated I felt.

HORACE. And Guy?

JUDY. Guy's an angel – affectionate, considerate. He might kill me with kindness.

HORACE. How's Jimi taking it all?

JUDY. He seems to like Guy, and Guy's very good with him.

HORACE. I meant Jerry. Does he understand?

JUDY. He keeps asking, 'Where's daddy? Where's daddy?' He gets hysterical and I don't know how to comfort him.

Pause.

What was that thing Jerry used to play?

HORACE. He played lots of things.

JUDY. It was a part of something . . . I can't remember.

HORACE. It was fun, though, wasn't it?

JUDY. What?

HORACE. That first summer.

JUDY. Was it? I'm not so sure. To be honest, it all seemed rather desperate. At least, it was for me.

HORACE. I thought we all had fun.

JUDY. It's too long ago.

She covers her face.

Jerry . . .

He looks at her, glances towards the kitchen, then at his watch.

HORACE. Can I get you anything?

She shakes her head and sits on the upright chair. It collapses beneath her.

Shit!

She cries like a child.

(*Helping her up.*) I'm so sorry.

GUY *enters with a platter of asparagus.*

GUY. The snack! Judy!

He rushes to her.

JUDY. I'm alright, alright . . .

HORACE. I've got to have that done.

GUY. Ma chérie!

JUDY. Shit!

She's quickly recovering her composure.

HORACE. I keep forgetting. Are you hurt?

JUDY. No, no, I'm alright.

HORACE. I keep meaning to –

JUDY. You've got to move, darling. This whole place is falling apart.

GUY. Ma petite.

HORACE. You're sure you're not hurt?

JUDY. I am not hurt, just slightly humiliated. Give me a drink.

HORACE does the honours as GUY comforts her.

GUY. I know what you want.

JUDY. What do I want?

GUY. A snack.

JUDY (*giggling*). You silly thing!

GUY takes an asparagus spear, dips the tip in mayonnaise and holds it by JUDY's mouth.

GUY. Just for you.

JUDY. Merci, monsieur.

Looking into GUY's eyes, she lets the spear slide into her mouth. HORACE checks his watch. She bites the spear and eats.

Mm. Now, that's what I call a snack.

The doorbell rings.

HORACE. Ah.

JUDY. Your friend.

HORACE. Excuse me.

He exits. GUY licks JUDY's lips clean.

GUY. Judy.

From the hallway, subdued voices.

JUDY. Dindon.

Enter HORACE *and* TERENCE.

Hello.

HORACE. This is . . .

TERENCE. Tebbit. Terence Tebbit.

JUDY. Terence.

She extends her hand.

Hello.

He shakes it.

I'm Judy and this is Guy.

TERENCE. Who?

GUY. Guy.

TERENCE. What's that, then?

HORACE. His name.

GUY (*shaking hands*). Enchanté.

TERENCE. Yeah.

GUY. You like a snack?

TERENCE. No. I'm alright, thanks.

HORACE. A glass of wine?

TERENCE. I'm alright.

GUY (*offering asparagus*). Horace, Judy . . .

HORACE (*taking a spear*). Thank you.

GUY (*raising glass*). À la vôtre!

JUDY. À la vôtre!

HORACE. À la –

TERENCE. Yeah.

They drink.

JUDY. So have you been together long?

HORACE. No. It's . . .

TERENCE. Not long.

HORACE. No.

JUDY. Well, I must say, Terence, you're frightfully well put together. You must work out an awful lot.

TERENCE. I try and keep my hand in.

JUDY. I bet you do. So where did you meet? Surely not at a gym. I can't imagine Horace in a gym.

HORACE. Well, we –

TERENCE. No, we didn't meet at a gym.

HORACE. No.

JUDY. I thought not.

TERENCE. No.

Beat.

HORACE (*to* TERENCE). So you . . . (*He doesn't know how to continue and takes a big glug of wine.*)

JUDY. It's so important, isn't it?

TERENCE. What's that?

JUDY. Keeping trim.

The phone rings. HORACE *goes to it.*

I work out five times a week –

HORACE (*answering phone*). Hello? . . .

JUDY. – and I feel great.

HORACE. Oh dear . . .

JUDY. So much more energy –

HORACE. Dear me . . .

JUDY. – and so much less stress.

HORACE (*offering her the phone*). It's Elvira.

JUDY. Jesus Christ!

She grabs it.

Yes? . . . What is it? . . . What? . . . Run away? Dear God in heaven, what am I paying you for, woman?!

She slams down the phone.

I knew I shouldn't have hired an Hispanic. We've got to go. Guy, on y va. (*To* TERENCE.) It's my little boy. He's a bit of a . . . (*Kissing* HORACE.) I'm sorry, darling.

HORACE. Don't worry.

JUDY. This is a complete disaster. Maybe on the way back from France we might find a spare twenty minutes –

HORACE. That'd be nice.

JUDY. – or whatever. We've really got to –

HORACE. You go. It's fine. We'll speak.

JUDY. I'll phone you tonight or –

HORACE. Yes.

JUDY (*to* TERENCE). It would have been so nice to have had a bit longer –

TERENCE. Yeah.

JUDY. Guy!

She's gone.

GUY (*grabbing a piece of asparagus. To* TERENCE).
Goodbye.

He goes.

HORACE. I'll . . .

HORACE *follows.* TERENCE *breathes a sigh of relief. He looks around. He goes on to the balcony and looks over. He comes back in as* HORACE *re-enters.*

I'm so sorry about that.

TERENCE. 'S'alright.

HORACE. I had no idea they were coming. They took me completely by surprise. In fact, when the door went, I thought it was you. Thanks for not . . . you know . . .

TERENCE. 'S'alright.

HORACE. I just thought it would be easier if . . . She's an old friend, you see. She lives in New York and that's her new – partner. I haven't seen her for years. Well, a few years – ago was the last time. I mean, I don't see her because I never go to – I never go over there. We met at school – not the same school, but we both knew – we had a mutual chum. Sorry, you don't need to know any of this.

TERENCE. 'S'alright.

HORACE. And they had a baby – the mutual chum and her – and I'm a godparent, so . . . I do hope Jimi'll be alright. Sorry, can I get you something? A drink, or – ?

TERENCE. No.

HORACE. Right.

Beat.

Funny how people can pop in and sort of . . . funny, isn't it?

TERENCE. This place . . .

HORACE. What?

TERENCE. Something about it.

HORACE. I've lived here a good many years. It belonged to my parents.

TERENCE. Something familiar.

HORACE. Really?

TERENCE. French, was he?

HORACE. Who?

TERENCE. That geezer.

HORACE. Yes, he was – is.

TERENCE. Fucking Frogs. No disrespect.

HORACE. No.

TERENCE. We used to call them tampons.

HORACE. Why?

TERENCE. Stuck-up cunts, aren't they?

HORACE. Oh, yes, I see.

TERENCE. Yeah. Anyway, where do you want to do it?

HORACE. Could we wait just a minute?

TERENCE *(checking his watch)*. If you like.

HORACE. I've – I've never done this before. Would you like
to sit down?

HORACE *moves the broken chair out of the way.*

Bit of an accident. Georgian. Late, I think.

TERENCE *sits on the sofa.* HORACE *hovers.* TERENCE
indicates for him to sit next to him. HORACE *does so.*

Would you like some music?

TERENCE. No.

Beat.

HORACE. Do I pay you before or – ?

TERENCE. Later. I might do a runner if you give me the dosh
now.

HORACE *(amused)*. Yes.

TERENCE. No, I might.

Beat.

HORACE. So your name's Terence.

TERENCE. Yeah.

HORACE. Right.

Beat.

Not Bronco.

...'s my trading name.

...ee.

. When I came in just now with them two here, I
– forgot myself, know what I mean?

HORACE. Yes, yes, I do. You carried it off enormously well.
Thank you.

TERENCE. 'S'alright.

Beat.

HORACE. What should I call you?

TERENCE. You don't have to call me nothing.

HORACE. Right. I'm Horace, by the way, should you want
to . . . call me something.

TERENCE. Yeah.

Beat.

HORACE. So have you been at it long?

TERENCE. About a year. Since I left the marines.

HORACE. You were a marine, were you?

TERENCE. Yeah.

HORACE. The agency said you'd been in uniform, but I didn't
pursue it. The marines. Gosh! How was that?

TERENCE. What?

HORACE. Well, being a marine.

TERENCE. 'S'alright. Made some good mates.

HORACE. Right.

TERENCE. Yeah.

HORACE. Why did you leave?

TERENCE. I finished my contract.

HORACE. Right. So did you go straight into . . . ?

TERENCE. Just about.

HORACE. Right.

TERENCE. And when I'm not shagging for a living, I do a bit of bouncing.

HORACE. Bouncing?

TERENCE. Yeah.

HORACE. Right. (*Penny dropping.*) Oh, as in 'bouncer'!

TERENCE. Yeah.

HORACE. So you manage to keep the wolf from the door?

TERENCE. I manage to keep him fucking miles from the door.

HORACE. Yes. Good.

TERENCE. Yeah. So what do you like?

HORACE. Ah, well –

TERENCE. I don't take it up the arse, right?

HORACE. Right.

TERENCE. And rimming's extra.

HORACE. Right.

Beat.

If we were to – get round to that, about – how much do you think – approximately?

TERENCE. Negotiable.

HORACE. Right.

TERENCE. Anything else, help yourself.

HORACE. Yes. Thank you.

TERENCE. You ever tried lenses?

HORACE. What's that?

TERENCE. Contact lenses.

HORACE. Oh, lenses! Yes, I have, as it happens, but I've got greasy tear-ducts. You think I should?

TERENCE. It's up to you, mate. I've seen you before.

HORACE. I don't think you have. Anyway, maybe –

TERENCE *puts his hand on* HORACE*'s knee.*

TERENCE. You alright?

HORACE. Yes, yes. It's just that . . . it's been quite a while.

TERENCE. Why's that?

HORACE. I don't know, really. I think about it, and occasionally get quite close to doing it, and it's – kind of worked out once or twice, but . . . To be honest, I'm not that experienced – at all.

TERENCE. What's so special about tonight, then?

HORACE. How do you mean?

TERENCE. Well, if you don't shag much, why've you suddenly decided to pay for it?

HORACE. Do you know, I don't know. Every now and again, I think I should do something about it, so I suppose that's what this is. I'm not the most adventurous person, but once in a while, I feel I ought to push the boat out.

TERENCE. There's nothing wrong with you, is there?

HORACE. No.

TERENCE. I'm not going to pull your knickers down and find you got a cunt and nine bollocks or nothing.

HORACE. No, no. I'm perfectly – you know.

TERENCE. That's weird.

HORACE. What is?

TERENCE. Not doing it much.

HORACE. Weird? Oh Christ, do you think I'm weird?

TERENCE. I don't know.

HORACE. Maybe I am. Maybe everyone thinks I'm weird. It's never crossed my mind before. Well, that's not strictly true.

TERENCE. Look, mate, no-one's saying you're weird. I'm just saying that not shagging much is weird, in that I have not met any geezer who has said that before. Right?

HORACE. Right.

TERENCE. Fucking hell!

HORACE. Sorry.

Beat.

Well, to be honest, I suppose there is a reason. It's because of someone else. I suppose I'm in love – in a manner of speaking.

TERENCE. You don't sound very sure.

HORACE. No, no, I am.

TERENCE. I mean, either you are or you're not, know what I mean?

HORACE. You're right, yes, and I am.

TERENCE. So why don't you shag him?

HORACE. He's dead.

TERENCE. Oh.

HORACE. He died about a year ago.

TERENCE. Oh.

HORACE. Blood-poisoning. Extraordinary, really. He cut himself – just a nick, a tiny nick – on one of those things that you – stick in paper – well, through paper that's got holes in it – do you know what I mean?

TERENCE. Yeah.

HORACE. – and it keeps it all together. Sort of – long silvery things that you put another silvery thing through with two prongs on it

TERENCE. I know what you mean –

HORACE. – that kind of flatten out when you –

TERENCE. Yeah. I know.

HORACE. Yes. Well, he nicked himself on one of those and got blood-poisoning and died . . . so quickly.

TERENCE. Probably rust.

HORACE. Yes. Extraordinary.

Beat.

Unfortunately, the silvery thing was holding together a manuscript of a novel I'd written. I so wanted him to read it, but he never got round to it because I gather that, when he took it out of the envelope – that's when he . . .

TERENCE. Nicked himself.

HORACE. Yes.

TERENCE. You a writer, then?

HORACE. No. Well, yes, but I don't earn a living from it. In fact, I don't earn anything from it. In fact, that novel's the only thing I've written. So far. And you, do you do it much – outside office hours, so to speak?

TERENCE. I haven't got anyone, if that's what you mean. So this dead bloke, knew him long, did you?

HORACE. Yes. We were at school together. He was the mutual chum I mentioned – of me and Judy.

TERENCE. You started early.

HORACE. Do you think so?

TERENCE. The first sex I had, outside the family, I was twenty-three.

HORACE. Ah no, I don't mean we –

TERENCE. What?

HORACE. Like – did anything, really – to speak of . . .

Beat.

Funny, isn't it?

TERENCE. Is it?

HORACE. Meeting like this.

TERENCE. We've met before.

HORACE. I don't think so.

TERENCE. We have, mate. I'm sure of it. What sort of guy do you like, then?

HORACE. Well, I suppose all sorts, really. I like you.

TERENCE. What was the bloke from school like?

HORACE. Jerry? Oh. He was . . .

TERENCE. You haven't forgotten, have you?

HORACE. No. Jerry was . . . I don't know. What sort of guy do you like?

TERENCE. Young.

HORACE. Young, yes, I like that, too. You're young, for goodness sake, and I'm not that old.

TERENCE. I mean, young.

HORACE. Uh-huh.

TERENCE. Really young.

HORACE. What, you mean . . . ?

TERENCE. Not toddlers, but – kids, you know.

HORACE. Uh-huh. That must be quite difficult.

TERENCE. You can always get one for a packet of fags, a couple of quid. No problem.

HORACE. Right.

TERENCE *picks up an asparagus spear and takes a bite.*

TERENCE (*throwing it down*). Ugh! Fucking horrible!

HORACE. Are you sure you wouldn't like a drink?

TERENCE. That what they eat in France, is it?

HORACE. Why don't I put on some music?

TERENCE. Whatever you like, mate.

He goes on to the balcony as HORACE *chooses a record
and puts it on: Beethoven's Fourth Piano Concerto, First
Movement. As the music starts, he hovers by the hi-fi.*

HORACE. Maybe not.

He takes it off. He looks at TERENCE, *then takes off his
glasses and pockets them. He goes on to the balcony and
stands next to* TERENCE, *who's looking at the view. They
don't touch.*

TERENCE. I lived near here as a kid.

HORACE. Really?

TERENCE (*pointing*). Yeah, over there. Still looks the fucking
same.

HORACE. The thing is – I'm really pleased to meet you. As
I say, I haven't done it for a while, and I really feel I'd like
to – with you.

HORACE *tentatively takes hold of* TERENCE*'s hand. Beat.
He rests his head on his shoulder.* TERENCE *pats*
HORACE*'s head.*

TERENCE. Fuck it.

He comes back into the room. HORACE *follows.*

HORACE. Sorry, have I – ?

TERENCE. It's not you, mate. I was just thinking . . . a mate
of mine. We was on duty once. Belfast. One minute, we was
talking, next minute, he's dead. Sniper. Don't even hear it.
Dead. Fuck it.

HORACE. I'm sorry.

TERENCE. It's what you're paid for.

HORACE. I suppose it is.

TERENCE. That's the way it goes, isn't it? You're shat into the
world, find there's a load of other poor cunts who didn't ask
to be here, work your bollocks off trying to get on with
them, then realise you're on your tod. Fucking joke, isn't it?

HORACE. Was your mate – was he . . . ?

TERENCE. We was good mates.

HORACE. Right.

TERENCE shows him a chain he's wearing around his neck.

TERENCE. This was his. We swapped chains after we'd been there for a bit. He gave me this and I gave him mine, one I'd had a good few years. It was sort of to mark the fact that we'd both survived the first five months. He didn't survive the sixth.

HORACE. It's funny, that guy I was telling you about, my friend from school, he gave me a chain.

TERENCE. Have you still got it?

HORACE. No, unfortunately. I misplaced it or something. Anyway . . .

TERENCE. Tell you what, let's call it a night.

HORACE. Oh.

TERENCE. I've lost it, know what I mean?

HORACE. Yes. Shame.

TERENCE. Sorry, mate. I won't charge you or nothing.

HORACE. No, it's not that – and I think you should. After all, you've made the effort to come here.

TERENCE. It's okay.

HORACE. Let me give you something at least.

He hands him a note.

TERENCE. Ta, mate. That's very decent of you.

HORACE. Perhaps we might make another date.

TERENCE. Yeah. You got the agency's number.

HORACE. Yes.

TERENCE (*patting HORACE's shoulder*). Cheers, mate. I'll see myself out.

HORACE. Cheers.

> TERENCE *leaves.* HORACE *is still. The front door is opened and shut. Pause. He goes to a drawer and takes out a Mars bar. He starts eating it. The phone rings. He swallows a mouthful and answers it.*

Hello? . . . Ah, yes. Hello . . . They left about a quarter of an hour ago . . . You've found him! Thank God for that! . . . On top of the wardrobe? . . . Oh dear. Well, you must keep your eye on him. They'll be back any minute now . . . Yes . . . Yes . . . Goodbye . . . Oh, er – adios – yes . . .

> *He puts down the phone and takes another bite. He thinks for a second, then puts the same piece of Beethoven back on: the opening of the Fourth Piano Concerto. He listens and takes another bite as the lights fade.*

SCENE TWO

Evening. The music continues. The doors onto the balcony are closed. A CD player has been added to the hi-fi. The broken chair is mended. HORACE, in an old shabby dressing-gown, is sprawled on the sofa, a glass of vodka in his hand, listening to the music, engrossed, his eyes closed. His glasses are on a side-table. The room is dark, lit by a single lamp. The door to the hall is closed. Light from the hall glows round the edge of the door. As the music reaches bar 50, the hall door slowly swings open, spreading light across the room. Silhouetted in the doorway is a YOUNG MAN. HORACE is oblivious. Pause.

YOUNG MAN. Excuse me.

No response.

Excuse me.

HORACE suddenly comes to with a yell and leaps to his feet.

HORACE. What the fuck – ?

YOUNG MAN. Sorry.

HORACE. What the fuck are you – ?

YOUNG MAN. Sorry.

HORACE. Who the fuck are you?

YOUNG MAN. I rang the bell.

HORACE (*grabbing his glasses and putting them on*). Get out.

YOUNG MAN. I'm sorry.

HORACE. Get out.

He stumbles to the CD player and turns off the music.

I'll call the police.

YOUNG MAN. No, don't.

HORACE (*picking up the receiver*). I will.

YOUNG MAN. Please don't.

HORACE. Then get the fuck out.

YOUNG MAN. Okay.

HORACE. Out!

YOUNG MAN. I'm going, alright?

HORACE. Now!

YOUNG MAN. Alright?

He doesn't move. HORACE suddenly freezes. He struggles to see the YOUNG MAN's face because the light's behind him. They stare at each other. Pause.

Are you Horace?

Beat. HORACE nods. He puts the phone down. He slowly approaches the YOUNG MAN. He switches on another lamp. We see the YOUNG MAN more clearly. He's seventeen, in school uniform, with a small rucksack on his shoulder. HORACE quietly gasps. Pause.

I'm Jimi.

Pause as they stare at each other.

I rang the bell a few times, then gave the door a push and it opened, so I came in. I didn't know what else to do. I'm sorry.

Beat.

I'll go, if you want.

Beat. JIMI holds out his hand to HORACE. For a moment HORACE can't move, then tentatively takes the outstretched hand. They don't shake, but keep hold of each other's hands for several seconds, eyes fixed on each other. Then:

Pleased to meet you.

HORACE. Jimi . . . (*Then he lets go of* JIMI's *hand, pulling himself together.*) I'm always forgetting to push the snib down. One day, someone'll just walk in and . . . I was floating away with the music. It was rather loud, I'm afraid, but I don't see the point of listening to Beethoven unless it's absolutely deafening. Oh God, everything's a terrible mess. Would you like a drink? I have to own up to being a bit pissed, actually. I'm trying to unlock the imagination. Vodka or – ?

JIMI. Thanks.

HORACE. How do you take it?

JIMI. However you take it.

HORACE. The last time I saw you – how old are you now?

JIMI. Seventeen.

HORACE. Seventeen. Shit! The last time I saw you, you were a little baby . . . a little baby . . .

He starts fixing the drinks.

Make yourself at home, please. Sit down, whatever. I'm sorry I wasn't more welcoming. How's your mother?

JIMI. She'll be alright.

HORACE. Where is she?

JIMI. I never know. Somewhere in Australia, I guess.

HORACE. Don't you live there now?

JIMI. She's based in Brisbane for a few years. I pop over in the holidays.

HORACE. So you're at school here?

JIMI. She thought I should do A-Levels in England, so she's had me transported to some dump in Hampshire. It's like Dotheboys Hall.

HORACE. Oh dear.

He hands him a drink.

JIMI. Thanks.

HORACE. Cheers.

JIMI. Cheers.

They drink.

HORACE. Would you like any food or – ?

JIMI. No, thank you.

HORACE. A bath or – I'm not saying you need one. I just mean, feel at home.

JIMI. Thanks. I'm fine.

HORACE. How long have you been here?

JIMI. Eighteen months.

HORACE. Gosh! Judy told me you were moving to Australia, but she didn't say you were coming here to school. Maybe it hadn't been sorted out. What a shame! We could have made contact before. Never mind. Why are you here?

JIMI. You're not angry, are you?

HORACE. Of course I'm not. I just want to know.

JIMI. I thought it was time we met. That's all.

Beat.

HORACE. Yes. Yes, good idea! So do you have – one of those things – oh, what are they called? – an exeat? That's it: exeat! God, I haven't used that word for a quarter of a century!

JIMI. Not exactly.

HORACE. You haven't run away, have you?

JIMI. Kind of.

HORACE. Oh.

JIMI. Sort of AWOL, for a bit.

HORACE. Oh.

They sip their vodka.

Jerry was – your dad was always in trouble. It was
ridiculous. I never was, of course. I was boringly well-
behaved, but Jerry! My God!

JIMI. That school, it's a waste of time, I tell you. But there's
no arguing with mummy.

HORACE. She's always been a bit like that.

JIMI. She thinks I'm not motivated, that there's nothing
driving me. She's scared I'll end up drifting.

HORACE. She's your mother. She's bound to worry, even if
there isn't anything to worry about. You're her sort of
masterpiece. Isn't that right?

JIMI. Bloody hell!

HORACE. Mothers are like that.

JIMI. 'The world belongs to those who know where they're
going,' that's what she says.

HORACE. There might be something in that.

JIMI. Do you know where you're going?

HORACE. Oh, no. I never go anywhere.

Beat.

I'm a bit thrown, actually, you being here like this. You
know you're quite like your father, don't you?

JIMI. Yes. I've seen photographs. I've seen one of you.

HORACE. Really?

JIMI. Well, I think it's you. There's dad as a teenager and this
other guy in glasses.

HORACE. Have you still got it?

JIMI. Yes. Mum was having a clear-out before we moved to
Oz, and I noticed it and kept it.

HORACE. You haven't got it with you, have you?

JIMI. No, but it's safe.

HORACE. Good.

JIMI *looks at the balcony.*

JIMI (*dawning realisation*). That's it, isn't it?

HORACE. What?

JIMI (*going to the balcony*). Where the photograph was taken.

He opens the doors and walks out.

You were standing here with that view behind you.

HORACE. Well, it wouldn't be exactly the same view –

JIMI. Incredible!

HORACE. I can't quite remember –

JIMI. You've been living here all this time?

HORACE. Yes.

JIMI. Christ! (*Re. the view.*) Oh, this is great. London, just lying there! Imagine, taking off and swooping across to Canary Wharf! Fantastic!

HORACE. It's a bit chilly, isn't it? I think you should come in. You'll catch cold.

JIMI *steps inside.* HORACE *shuts the doors.*

JIMI. Have you still got the beads?

HORACE. Beads?

JIMI. That you were wearing in the photograph.

HORACE. I was wearing beads?

JIMI. You looked pretty weird.

HORACE. Oh dear.

JIMI. Still, I suppose that was the fashion.

HORACE. Was your dad wearing beads?

JIMI. No. He was wearing a chain.

HORACE. Of course he was. God, that chain! He gave it me, you know.

JIMI. Did he? Have you still got it?

HORACE. No. It disappeared. One minute I had it, the next minute it had gone. I can't tell you how upset I was.

Beat.

What was the name of . . . ? Guy, that's it! What happened to Guy?

JIMI. Who?

HORACE. Your mum had a French friend called Guy.

JIMI. I don't know who you're talking about.

HORACE. You all lived together for a while. Don't you remember? In New York.

JIMI. Oh, hang on a minute, yes. He cooked a lot or something.

HORACE. That sounds like Guy.

JIMI. And she found him having it off with some foreign bird in the kitchen.

HORACE. Oh dear.

JIMI. I guess that was the end of him. Mum enjoys her independence, but doesn't much enjoy anybody else's. He died not long after that. Apparently he choked on something he'd cooked.

HORACE. My God!

JIMI. Got a feather stuck in his throat, I think mum said.

HORACE. Poor Guy.

JIMI. She didn't seem too bothered.

HORACE. You're being a bit hard on her.

JIMI. It's the truth. Mum's got through a few blokes in her time. They pass through so quickly, it's hardly worth getting to know them.

HORACE. Now, come on.

JIMI. She gets bored, that's all.

HORACE. Why are you here?

JIMI. I've told you.

HORACE. Tell me again.

JIMI. I wanted to meet you. You're my godfather. You knew
my dad.

HORACE. But why have you gone to all this trouble? You
could have got my number, we could have arranged to meet.

Beat.

JIMI. I had a dream last night. I was in a garden – something
like a garden – and it felt like home. I was looking around,
and then dad was there standing next to me. He asked if I
was alright and I said yes, and I asked if he was alright and
he said yes, and he gave me a smile, and then I woke up. I
tried to go back to sleep and pick up where I left off, but
that never works, does it? I wanted to meet you, the guy my
dad had his arm round in that picture, the two of you
looking like cats that got the cream.

HORACE. What did your dad look like in the dream?

JIMI. Like that. Like the photo.

Beat.

HORACE. Would you like another?

JIMI *nods.* HORACE *takes his glass and fixes two more
drinks.* JIMI *takes out a pack of cigarettes.*

JIMI. Do you mind?

HORACE. No.

JIMI. Do you want one?

HORACE. Why not?

JIMI *offers him one.*

Thanks.

JIMI *lights their cigarettes.* HORACE *hands him his drink.*

JIMI. So what was he like?

HORACE. Who?

JIMI. My dad.

HORACE. Your dad was . . . he was great.

JIMI. You met at school?

HORACE. Yes. We became aware of each other when we were about sixteen. He'd mixed with other boys before that, a different crowd than what I used to hang out with. Actually, we'd come into contact a few years before in a school play, one of those mystery things – The Creation. He was The Serpent.

JIMI. What were you?

HORACE. Eve.

JIMI. How did you manage that?

HORACE. I was in a flesh-coloured body-stocking with a fig-leaf. But we didn't really have that much to do with each other. I think he thought I was a bit – a bit of a poof. In fact, I know he did, because he used to say things like, 'You're a bit of a poof, aren't you?' But I didn't really mind because he was at that age when boys can be like that, but a few years later . . . he'd changed. It was probably all to do with puberty and everything, but he was – really nice to me and we became mates. It was music, really. He was a very good musician.

JIMI. I know.

HORACE. Truly gifted. He arranged a concert once. Lots of people were involved and he played some fantastic stuff. But I'll always remember, he got a couple of trebles, really quite young, to sing this duet by Monteverdi. It was most inappropriate, lyrics-wise, but that was Jerry for you: always chancing his arm.

JIMI. Why was it inappropriate?

HORACE. They were declaring undying love to each other, and they were eleven. Still, there were no complaints, probably because it was in Italian. It was the most exquisite moment. These pure voices, with Jerry accompanying them on piano. It was the only time I saw him lost for words.

Beat. JIMI goes out onto the balcony. HORACE hovers, then steps out next to him.

JIMI. Don't you ever feel you could raise yourself even a few inches off the ground, and glide, glide away?

HORACE. To be honest, no.

The nearby church clock starts striking the hour very loudly.

JIMI. Jesus!

HORACE. Sorry.

Stroke two.

I've had to live with this for years –

Stroke three.

You kind of get used to it.

Stroke four.

JIMI. Jesus!

HORACE. It is a bit –

Stroke five.

– loud, I know, but –

Stroke six.

– it'll be over in a –

Stroke seven.

– second or two.

JIMI. I've run away.

Stroke eight.

HORACE. What?

JIMI. I've run away.

He comes back in as the clock strikes for the ninth and final time. HORACE steps inside and shuts the balcony doors. JIMI starts pacing restlessly.

HORACE. You said.

JIMI. What?

HORACE. You've already told me you've run away.

JIMI. Yeah.

HORACE. For a bit.

JIMI. That's right, yeah.

HORACE. Yes. Are you alright?

JIMI. Yeah.

HORACE. God, it's cold out there!

JIMI. Did you and dad ever take drugs?

HORACE. No.

JIMI. Didn't you?

HORACE. Not that I remember.

JIMI. You look like you did.

HORACE. What do you mean?

JIMI. In the picture.

HORACE. Oh. Well, we might have had a – little something or other.

JIMI. Would you like a little something or other now?

HORACE. What are you talking about?

JIMI (*taking out a little packet*). Would you like a little something now?

HORACE. I'm really not sure whether –

JIMI. This guy at school, he's always got a little something or other. He's one of Lord Charlecote's sons. (*Undoing the packet.*) Would you like some?

HORACE. You shouldn't be taking that. What is it?

JIMI. Coke.

HORACE. Well, you shouldn't be taking it. You shouldn't be taking anything. You shouldn't be smoking, for goodness sake!

JIMI. Would you like some?

HORACE. And are you sure you need any? You've been a bit
jumpy all evening.

JIMI. Would you?

HORACE (*with a barely discernible nod*). Mm.

   JIMI *starts organising the coke.* HORACE *hovers.*

   It's so nice seeing you without a lump on your head – God,
   I'm sorry!

JIMI. What?

HORACE. You used to have one as a baby, (*Indicating the
   middle of the forehead.*) right there. You didn't know, did
   you?

JIMI. No.

HORACE. God, I am sorry. Jerry thought you were from
   another planet. He said it was an implanted radio to receive
   messages from your mother-ship.

JIMI. I don't think I've seen any photographs of me as a baby.

HORACE. Sorry.

JIMI. What happened to it?

HORACE. It went, apparently, of its own accord. It seems
   these things come and go. I didn't mean to . . . I'm sorry.

JIMI. No problem.

   JIMI *chopping the coke,* HORACE *watching.*

HORACE. That was the last time I saw Jerry.

JIMI. When?

HORACE. Your christening, which was the first time I saw
   you. We had a great time, your dad and me. Not at the
   christening. Well, it was alright, as christenings go – not
   that I've been to many – any, really – oh, well, one or two.
   But when we were younger – your dad – your dad was
   everything that was – happy and good then – at that time in
   my life, and which has gone now – like him. There was one

day, one day we had – when I met your mother, actually – which was sort of complete. One of those moments in life when you realise, 'Ah, that's what it's like to be happy.' I hoped there'd be more days like that, but there weren't. Not quite like that, anyway. When I'm dying, it's that moment that'll make me think it was all worthwhile. My life crystallized in the memory of a moment. It was like we were outside time.

JIMI. How long's a moment?

HORACE. It's not a minute or a second. It's a mystery. A moment is part of the mystery of life.

JIMI. You're not dying, are you?

HORACE. No.

JIMI. Are you?

HORACE. I'm perfectly well.

JIMI. You're not ill?

HORACE. No. I'm perfectly well. Why do you ask?

JIMI. Have you got a note?

HORACE. What?

JIMI. I've only got a scrunched-up fiver.

HORACE. Right. (*Looking through his wallet.*) Do you need some? I mean, apart from –

JIMI. No.

HORACE. Sure?

JIMI. Well, I suppose the odd spare quid always comes in handy.

HORACE *takes out a £50 note hands it to* JIMI.

HORACE. Keep it.

JIMI. No, no –

HORACE. It's yours.

JIMI. Brilliant!

JIMI *rolls up the note.*

HORACE. Actually, I have had this before – once – in the museum basement – with an Egyptologist.

JIMI. Did you like it?

HORACE. I liked the Egyptologist.

JIMI *offers him the rolled note.* HORACE *looks at the coke.*

JIMI. A quatrain of cocaine.

HORACE. What do you mean?

JIMI. Four lines.

HORACE. Very good.

He snorts.

(*Passing the note to* JIMI.) Thank you.

JIMI *snorts a line.*

I've always wondered what it was like to be a godparent.
So.

JIMI. So, Horace. You don't mind me calling you that, do you?

HORACE. It's my name.

JIMI (*giggling*). I know.

He goes out on to the balcony.

HORACE. Oh dear. Not again.

JIMI. Oh, Horace!

HORACE (*following him out*). Isn't it too cold for this?

JIMI (*holding out his arms to the view*). Horace, Horace, wouldn't it be great to fly?

HORACE. Not too loud, Jimi.

JIMI. To take off and fucking fly!

HORACE. Is this the coke talking?

JIMI. No, I've always wanted to fly. Look at the moon, Horace!

HORACE. Yes.

JIMI. What a fucking lovely moon!

HORACE. Jimi, you must keep your voice down.

JIMI. The mooniest fucking moon I ever did see!

HORACE (*momentarily thrown*). What did you say?

JIMI. Wow! This is great, Horace. Let's have another drink.

HORACE. You really mustn't catch cold.

He comes back in and starts fixing drinks.

JIMI. I want to be a planet, Horace –

HORACE. Oh, God!

JIMI. I want to be part of the planetary system.

HORACE. Jimi –

JIMI. I want to be a part of history!

HORACE (*to himself*). Horace, why are you feeling tense?
Why are you feeling so tense? Oh, fuck it!

He takes the glasses and vodka bottle on to the balcony.

Help yourself.

JIMI. I want something to fight for.

HORACE. Want, want, want.

JIMI. Don't you, Horace? Don't you want something to fight
for, Horace?

HORACE. You don't have to keep saying my name.

JIMI. Something to believe in. That'd be great, wouldn't it,
Horace? And to have somebody – have somebody to believe
in. That's the thing! To have someone to grow strong with. I
mean, not everyone lets you down, do they?

HORACE. Let's go in.

JIMI. Have you got anyone, Horace?

HORACE. It's cold, Jimi.

JIMI. Have you?

HORACE. Let's go in.

He waits for JIMI *to step past him, then comes in himself and shuts the doors.*

Are you sure you're not hungry?

JIMI. Yeah, yeah, I'm fine.

He's rolling up the note again.

HORACE. Do you think you should?

JIMI. Horace, we've hardly started. Enjoy yourself.

He hands HORACE *the note.*

HORACE. Yes. Yes, maybe you're right.

He snorts, then hands the note back to JIMI.

Thank you.

JIMI *snorts.*

JIMI. I've done a bit of writing, you know.

HORACE. Good.

JIMI. You have, too, haven't you?

HORACE. No.

JIMI. I thought you'd written a novel.

HORACE. Ah, the novel, yes. That was years ago.

JIMI. What was it about?

HORACE. This and that.

JIMI. What?

HORACE. Obsessive desire. Bleeding humanity. The tragic inexplicability of existence. The usual.

JIMI. Can I read it?

HORACE. Yes, yes, you can. I'll dig out a copy for you. Actually, Judy's probably got one, or maybe it didn't survive the clear-out. No, I'll get you one.

JIMI (*toasting with the vodka*). Cheers.

HORACE. Cheers.

They drink.

Jimi.

JIMI. Yes?

HORACE. Why did you tell me you'd run away?

JIMI. Cos I have.

HORACE. I mean, why did you tell me again?

JIMI. I don't know.

He downs the rest of his vodka.

It's hard, though, isn't it, writing?

HORACE. It is.

JIMI. I wonder what the secret is?

HORACE. If there is a secret, I don't know it. Having ideas and expressing them, that's writing for you. I'm the last person to ask.

Beat.

I read somewhere that you must always remember that no two things are the same, exactly the same: no two roses, no two worms, no two apples or birds or grains of sand, no two things are ever exactly alike, and you must be able to distinguish each clearly and accurately. I read that somewhere or other. Does that help? No two hairs or cells of skin are ever indistinguishable. No two hands, fingers, thumbs or nails, chins, eyebrows, ears . . . You are so like him.

JIMI. What?

HORACE. Your hair, your eyes, your nose – lips . . . When I saw you, for a second, I thought you were him.

Pause.

It's wearing me out.

Pause. JIMI *goes over to the piano and sits on the stool.*

*Music is open on the stand. He starts sightreading, with
great difficulty, the opening of Beethoven's Fourth Piano
Concerto. HORACE is taken aback. As JIMI struggles with
the music, HORACE goes over and stands behind him.
JIMI stops playing for a moment, then continues. Eventually
HORACE raises a hand, intending to touch JIMI's hair.
Before contact is made, JIMI stops playing again.
HORACE takes his hand away as JIMI takes his hands
from the keys. HORACE freezes. JIMI suddenly throws his
arms around HORACE's waist and buries his face in his
belly.*

Jimi . . . Jimi . . .

It seems JIMI's crying.

Jimi, what's wrong? What is it? What's wrong?

*JIMI suddenly gets up and starts pacing in an effort to keep
control.*

What is it?

*JIMI paces himself to a standstill, his hands covering his
face.*

Tell me, Jimi. Please.

JIMI. He told me . . .

HORACE. Yes?

JIMI. He told me this morning . . .

HORACE. Yes?

JIMI. . . . before prayers that . . .

HORACE. What?

JIMI. That that's it.

HORACE. Oh.

JIMI. It's over.

HORACE. Who told you this?

JIMI. Poppy.

HORACE. Who's Poppy?

JIMI. The cunt I've fallen in love with.

HORACE. Poppy?

JIMI. It's a nickname. We've all got them.

HORACE. Right.

JIMI. I'm sorry. Forget it. I didn't mean to –

HORACE. There's nothing to be sorry about. Tell me about him. Tell me about Poppy.

JIMI. Well – he appeared about – six months ago – exactly six months ago – and we hit it off, just like that. I'd played around, as you do, even had a few girlfriends, but Poppy – well . . .

Beat.

It was him who started it all. He made the first move. We were doing a cross-country run, jogging along together, having a bit of a chat, and he suddenly stopped and said, 'Why don't you kiss me?', so I did, and from that moment to – to this morning, we haven't stopped.

Beat.

He's kind of completely taken me over. It's been incredible; the best – the very best time of my life, and now . . .

HORACE. You've no idea why he'd say that that's it?

JIMI. No, no, I don't. It doesn't make sense. When he spoke to me today, there was nothing – nothing in his eyes – nothing to acknowledge what we'd . . . He's the only thing, Horace, that's meant anything. If that is it, then I don't see the point.

HORACE. I'm sorry. That's a terrible thing to –

JIMI. People always let you down, don't they?

HORACE. Well –

JIMI. Give up on you, die on you, always fucking let you down.

HORACE. I'm not sure that's always –

JIMI. What the fuck am I going to do?

The phone rings. Neither of them moves. It continues ringing. HORACE *picks up the receiver.*

HORACE. Hello? . . . Judy! What a surprise! . . .

JIMI frantically indicates that he doesn't want her to know he's there.

Is everything alright? . . . What's happened? . . . Yes? . . . He's at school here? . . . I didn't know that . . . Run away? . . . No, he's not here. Why on earth would he be? . . . Well, I think that's a bit extreme . . . Look, boys of his age, you know what they're like. He'll probably turn up in next to no time . . . Yes. I think the headmaster's right: leave it till morning and see what happens . . . Where are you? . . . Yes, Brisbane'd be nice . . . I'll think about it . . . Yes, I'll phone a few travel agents . . . Okay . . . Lovely to hear from you . . . Bye.

He puts the phone down. JIMI*'s started pacing round the room.*

JIMI. Wouldn't you bloody know it?

HORACE. She phoned the school, just to say hello, I think, and the headmaster obviously had to tell her you weren't there.

JIMI. Wouldn't you just bloody know it?

HORACE. He sounds like a decent bloke because she was saying he ought to call the police and he thought it wasn't necessary – yet. So I reckon if you turn up sometime tomorrow or – whenever . . . Would you like something to eat?

JIMI, still pacing, doesn't seem to hear. HORACE *goes to a drawer and takes out two Mars bars. He offers one to* JIMI.

JIMI. Thanks.

They unwrap their bars and start eating them. JIMI *paces intermittently.* HORACE *starts to as well.*

So what do you think, Horace? It's a joke, isn't it?

HORACE. Well, it's . . .

Beat.

It's very difficult.

JIMI. I know that.

HORACE. I think it's fair to say that I do understand how important – Poppy is to you and how – awful it must be for you at the moment, but I think it's also fair to say that, in time, the chances are that you'll meet someone else who could mean as much, if not more to you than Poppy does now.

Beat.

So maybe the best thing would be to – would be to forget him.

Pause.

But then again . . .

Beat.

JIMI. There won't be anyone else. I don't want anyone else. I want him. Do you understand that?

HORACE. Yes.

JIMI. I want him.

JIMI's *foot goes through a floorboard. He yells in pain.*

HORACE (*rushing to him*). Jesus!

JIMI. Fuck!

HORACE. Are you alright?

JIMI. Fuck in fucking hell!

HORACE (*trying to release his foot*). Does it hurt?

JIMI. Of course it fucking hurts!

HORACE. Gently does it . . .

HORACE *very carefully releases his foot.*

There we go.

JIMI. Fuck!

HORACE. There's a bit of blood. Let's sit you over here and I'll put something on it.

He helps JIMI *to the upright chair and carefully sits him down. The chair collapses beneath him and he falls to the floor.*

Oh, God! What the fuck am I doing?

JIMI *bursts out laughing.*

Jimi, I'm so sorry. I've been meaning to get that bloody chair done for –

JIMI *gets hysterical. He starts to roll around the floor. HORACE watches and smiles.*

Do you know – your mum – your mum sat on that years ago and it – it did the same thing!

JIMI (*clutching his crutch*). Shit, I've wet myself!

HORACE *starts to giggle.*

I've fucking wet myself!

HORACE. I could get you a change of – if you'd like –

JIMI. Eh, Horace – Horace –

HORACE. What?

JIMI. I've really put my foot in it this time, haven't I?

This finishes him off. HORACE *looks at him, then glances at the hole in the floorboard. He freezes, staring at the hole.*

You'll have to move, Horace – only thing for it.

HORACE *reaches into the hole and takes out a gold chain. He holds it up and looks at it, amazed.* JIMI *eventually notices this. He crawls to* HORACE *and also looks at the chain.*

Dad's?

HORACE *nods.* JIMI *delicately touches the chain.*

Dad . . .

Pause. Then HORACE *kneels behind* JIMI *and fastens the chain around his neck. He retrieves his Mars bar and resumes eating it.* JIMI *gets up and looks in a mirror. He touches the chain. He goes over to* HORACE *and stands above him. Beat.* JIMI *very tentatively places a hand on* HORACE's *head, then gently strokes his hair. Beat.* HORACE *very gently lets his head rest against* JIMI's *thigh. The lights fade.*

SCENE THREE

*It's a summer afternoon. The balcony doors are open. A fair
can be heard in the distance. Some of the furniture is stacked
against walls. A tea-chest remains unpacked. The floor is bare.
There's a dansette and a stack of records. An acoustic guitar
leans against the piano. HORACE, aged 17, is looking in a
mirror putting on a string of beads. He's wearing gold-rimmed
National Health spectacles and a few bracelets and badges,
including a military medal on a ribbon. He studies himself. He
decides to take off the beads. He dashes on to the balcony and
looks out. Beat. He dashes back in. He checks himself in the
mirror again. The beads go back on. He puts the stylus on a
record already on the turntable: 'Strange Orchestras' by
Tyrannosaurus Rex. He starts moving to it and then tries to
sing along. The door is pushed open revealing JERRY, aged 17.
HORACE hasn't noticed him. JERRY stands watching for a
while, then:*

JERRY (*singing with the record*). 'Then they giggle and they
    wiggle through the door in the big dark oak tree.'

  HORACE *spins round, covered in confusion.*

HORACE. Hi.

JERRY. Hi.

  HORACE *takes the record off.*

  Steve Peregrine Took on pixiephone.

HORACE. Yeah. Hi.

JERRY. Hi. The door was open.

HORACE. Oh, right. I must remember to push the snib down.
    Mum and dad'll kill me. You found it alright, then.

JERRY. Yeah. It's cool.

HORACE. Yeah. I'll show you round, shall I?

JERRY. Yeah, yeah, later.

HORACE. Yeah.

JERRY (*going on to the balcony*). Great view! That's amazing!

HORACE. Yeah.

JERRY. Amazing! It makes a change from Edmonton, I bet.

HORACE. Yeah, although I quite liked Edmonton. I'd have been happy to stay there.

JERRY. But you've got the whole of London at your feet!

HORACE. Yes. It is nice, I must say.

JERRY. It's great.

HORACE. Yeah.

Beat.

Mum and dad are away. They needed a break after the move. They're not coming back till tomorrow, so we've got the whole place to ourselves, if we want.

JERRY. Great!

HORACE. Yeah.

JERRY. We could go to the fair.

HORACE. Yeah, yeah, we could.

JERRY (*coming back in*). And a piano! Fantastic!

He plays a ten-second boogie.

Great!

HORACE. Yeah. Do you want anything?

JERRY. What have you got?

HORACE. I've got some pop.

JERRY. What sort?

HORACE. Dandelion and burdock.

JERRY. I'll wait.

HORACE. Right. Oh, by the way, I've finished with your 'Hobbit', if you want it back.

JERRY. Have you read it?

HORACE. Mm.

JERRY. What do you think?

HORACE. It's good, yeah.

JERRY. You didn't like it, did you?

HORACE. I did.

JERRY. You didn't. I can tell.

HORACE. I did.

JERRY. You didn't, Horace.

HORACE. Well, I didn't get it, really.

JERRY. It's easy.

HORACE. I don't mean like that. I mean, like, I don't get gnomes and things.

JERRY. It's not just gnomes, mate.

HORACE. Isn't it?

JERRY. No.

HORACE. Well, I'm afraid I couldn't see beyond the gnomes. That's all I got: gnomes.

JERRY. And anyway, they're not gnomes; they're dwarves.

HORACE. Are they?

JERRY. Yeah. Read it again.

HORACE. Again?

JERRY. Give it another go.

HORACE. You think I should?

JERRY. Yeah, cos once you get into it – wow!

HORACE. Right. I'll hang on to it, then, shall I?

JERRY. Yeah.

HORACE. Right.

He takes a slightly bent untipped cigarette from his pocket.

Look.

JERRY. Great!

HORACE. Park Drive. I nicked it from dad.

JERRY takes out a packet of ten No. 6.

JERRY. Nicked from the newsagent down the road.

HORACE. Great! So we're alright for fags.

JERRY. Yeah, and Jude rolls her own, so we're well in.

HORACE. Who?

JERRY. Jude. Judy.

HORACE. Who's Judy?

JERRY. She's this girl I met a week or so ago from the girls'
    school. Her family's just moved down from the Midlands.
    She's incredible.

HORACE. You never said.

JERRY. It's only just happened.

HORACE. And she's coming here?

JERRY. Yeah, any minute now. It's alright, isn't it? She's really
    cool. You'll love her.

HORACE. Will I?

JERRY. Yeah, she's fantastic.

HORACE. Great!

JERRY. I'll tell you something, Horry, she can't get enough
    of it.

HORACE. Can't she?

JERRY. No.

HORACE. Enough of what?

JERRY. You know . . .

HORACE. You've done it with her?

JERRY. Yeah. On our first date.

HORACE. Gosh.

JERRY. And I'll tell you something else: (*Confidentially.*) she sucks like a dream.

HORACE. Does she?

JERRY. Yeah. She can get the whole thing into her mouth.

HORACE. Gosh.

JERRY. Right up to the pubes, and she says next time she's going to try and get my balls in as well. Can you imagine?

HORACE. She must have a big mouth, then.

JERRY. You've got to give it a go, Horace.

HORACE. What, you mean . . . you want me . . . you want me to – ?

JERRY. A bit of mutual's okay, but sinking your prick into pussy – fuck!

HORACE. Oh. Right.

JERRY. You've just got to do it.

HORACE. Yes. I'll think about it.

JERRY. Absolutely definitely, old mate. Take it from me. (*Noticing guitar*). Fantastic!

JERRY *picks up the guitar and starts tuning it.* HORACE *hovers, then wanders on to the balcony. Out of* JERRY*'s eyeline, he mouths 'Fuck, fuck, fuck,' full of angst.* JERRY, *oblivious, starts strumming, then sings a slow version of 'To Love Somebody'.* HORACE *is breathing deeply in an effort to calm himself. He turns to look at* JERRY *and becomes entranced.*

(*Singing.*) 'There's a light, a certain kind of light,
That never shone on me.
I want my life to be
Lived with you, lived with you.
There's a way, everybody say,
To do each and every little thing.
But what does it bring,
If I ain't got you, ain't got you . . .

Unnoticed by either, JUDY, aged 16, has appeared in the doorway with a shoulder-bag. She can't see HORACE. She stands watching JERRY. Eventually, he spots her. He doesn't stop singing and performs for her.

'Hey baby, you don't know what it's like,
Baby, you don't know what it's like
To love somebody, to love somebody,
The way I love you.'

At first, HORACE can't work out what's going on, then steps inside and notices her. JERRY breaks off.

JERRY (*to* JUDY). Hi.

JUDY (*to* JERRY). Hi.

HORACE. Hi.

JERRY. This is Horace.

JUDY. Hi.

HORACE. Hi.

JERRY. Judy.

HORACE. Right.

JUDY. Yeah. Hi.

HORACE. Hi.

JUDY. You can call me Jude.

HORACE. Right.

JUDY. Yeah. Got anything to drink?

HORACE. Dandelion and burdock.

JUDY. Fuck. I've just had some Dimyril, see, and I'm a bit –

The church clock starts striking the hour loudly.

JERRY. Fuck me!

HORACE. Yeah. They didn't tell us about this –

Stroke two.

– when we came to view it.

JUDY. Wow!

Stroke three.

This fucking Dimyril, man! I can hear a sort of –

Stroke four – the last.

Wow! (*Subsiding into* JERRY *and closing her eyes.*) Mmm . . . baby, baby . . .

JERRY. Where is it?

Eyes still closed, she fumbles in her bag and takes out a medicine bottle. JERRY *takes it from her.*

HORACE. What's Dimyril?

JERRY. An expectorant.

HORACE. Has she got a cough?

JERRY (*unscrewing the cap*). Not after half a bottle.

He takes a swig and offers it to HORACE. *He takes the bottle and eyes it suspiciously as* JUDY *lifts her open mouth to* JERRY's. *They kiss with great passion.* HORACE *takes a swig. It tastes disgusting. He watches them kissing for a while, then takes another swig. He starts looking through his records and puts on the title track of the LP 'Are You Experienced?' by Jimi Hendrix.*

JUDY (*breaking from the kiss*). Oh, yeah! Jimi, Jimi . . .

JERRY. Got a roll-up?

She hands him her bag, grooving to the music. HORACE *starts grooving in a minor way.*

JUDY. Oh, Jimi . . . I saw his trousers split in Coventry. Amazing!

JERRY*'s taken out a small tin.*

There's some grass in there if you want.

JERRY. Yeah. Beautiful.

He starts rolling a joint.

Hey, Horry, what about that bastard Eccleston, eh? I mean, what a bastard!

HORACE. I don't have that much to do with him.

JERRY. He had the cheek to say to me – listen to this – the bare-faced cheek to say that, without a doubt, the best riff the Stones have ever done is 'Mother's Little Helper'. 'Mother's Little Helper'! I said, 'That's not a proper riff, Eccleston, let alone a good one.' I said, 'You wouldn't know a decent riff if it came up and bit you on your fat arse.'

HORACE. I quite like 'Mother's Little Helper'.

JERRY. The song's not at issue; it's the riff.

JUDY*'s started half-squatting up and down, slowly, arms half-raised, in time to the music.*

JUDY. Every time I hear the Stones, I just – well up, you know? Beautiful Brian, dead as fuck. I loved Brian . . . Harry.

JERRY. Horry.

JUDY. Yeah, I really loved him. I reckon he's floating around, floating around up there, being beautiful just for us.

HORACE. So which one do you think's best?

JERRY. Obvious: 'Jumpin' Jack Flash.'

HORACE. Yeah, I suppose so. I like 'Have You Seen Your Mother, Baby.'

JERRY. I'm not talking about songs; I'm talking about riffs.

HORACE. Good, though, isn't it?

JERRY. Jude, what are you doing?

JUDY (*half-squatting dreamily*). I'm leaping with Armstrong . . . moondancing with Jimi . . . fantastic . . .

JERRY *licks the paper and seals the joint.*

JERRY. Got a light?

HORACE. Yeah.

He hands him the matches. JERRY *lights up and inhales.*

JERRY. Mmm. Beautiful . . .

He hands it to HORACE, *who takes a drag.* JERRY *lies on the floor and puts his legs up against a wall at a right-angle, his arms behind his head.* HORACE *passes the joint to* JUDY, *then goes to the record-player. He takes off the LP and puts on a single: 'The Wind Cries Mary.'*

JUDY (*on hearing the intro*). Yeah . . .

She lies on her stomach, her face next to JERRY's. *Their position evokes a still of James Dean and Natalie Wood in 'Rebel Without a Cause'. She holds the joint for him to drag on. He does so. Then she has another drag, puts her lips over his and blows the smoke into his mouth.* HORACE *stands watching.*

HORACE. That's what they did in 'Pierrot Le Fou'.

JERRY. What?

HORACE. Smoke like that.

JUDY. No, they didn't.

HORACE. They did.

JERRY. You're on dodgy ground, Horry. This girl is in love with Belmondo.

JUDY. And you, baby . . . (*Kissing him.*)

HORACE. I'm sure they did.

JUDY. Jean-Paul, Jean-Paul . . .

She kisses him again.

HORACE. I'm right, aren't I, Jerry?

JERRY. Ah, mon petit potiron.

JUDY (*feeling his crotch*). Oh, monsieur, qu'est-ce que c'est?

JERRY. La plume de ma tante.

HORACE. Aren't I?

JUDY. Ooh la la!

They kiss again, HORACE *watching.* JERRY *clocks him over her shoulder.*

JERRY. So who do you like, Horry?

HORACE. In what way?

JERRY. Film stars. Which ones flick your switch?

HORACE. I don't know. No-one, really.

JERRY. There must be someone.

HORACE. Well, there are people I like watching. Rita Tushingham – she can be good, Albert Finney, Hayley Mills –

JERRY. Hayley Mills?

HORACE. Yes.

JERRY. Hayley fucking Mills?

JUDY. Who the fuck's Hayley Mills?

JERRY. 'Let's get together, yeah, yeah, yeah . . . '

HORACE. I know she's a bit passé –

JERRY. A bit? She must be over twenty by now!

HORACE. But something like 'Whistle Down The Wind' – I really rate that, and she was great. I reckon that film'll survive us all.

JERRY. What are you talking about?

HORACE. Really stand the test of time, you know?

JERRY *starts giggling.*

What is it?

JERRY. It's just dawned on me.

JUDY. What, baby?

JERRY. If you sucked off Belmondo, you'd have a frog in your throat.

He carries on giggling. Then JUDY *gets it and starts giggling too.*

A frog in your throat.

They get hysterical. HORACE *doesn't.*

Then you'd really need your Dimyril.

Ongoing hysteria. HORACE *goes over to them.*

HORACE. Can I have some more, please?

They haven't heard. HORACE *takes the joint from* JUDY *and smokes it. Their hysteria subsides into a snog.* JERRY *starts undoing her jeans. She helps him.* HORACE *watches, dragging on the joint.* JERRY *puts his hand down the front of her jeans.*

JERRY. Mmm . . . yeah . . . my favourite hobbit-hole.

They kiss.

You're not going to believe this, but I know somebody who doesn't get 'The Hobbit'.

JUDY. What?

JERRY. Thinks it's about gnomes.

They kiss.

JUDY. It is about gnomes.

JERRY *rolls on top of her. He puts his hands up her top and fondles her breasts. She moans.* HORACE *watches in increasing discomfort.* JERRY *works down her body, kissing her navel, then licking beneath it. As he starts to inch her jeans down, she snores. He looks up at her face.*

She's out for the count. He smiles at HORACE. HORACE doesn't return the smile and goes on to the balcony. By now, 'The Wind Cries Mary' has finished. JERRY gets to his feet. He wanders on to the balcony.

JERRY. She's crazy. She's something else.

Beat.

What's wrong?

HORACE. Nothing.

JERRY. Have I said something?

HORACE *shakes his head.*

Mm, that sun. So warm. The sunniest fucking sun I ever did see!

Beat.

It's not about 'The Hobbit', is it?

HORACE. No.

Beat.

JERRY. We should go to the fair.

HORACE. Yeah.

JERRY. Horace, tell me. Come on. Don't get sad. It's a nice day. We're having a nice day.

A luxurious snore from JUDY.

HORACE. I just think . . .

JERRY. What?

HORACE. That you could've told me – about Judy.

JERRY. I didn't know she was coming till the last minute.

HORACE. I didn't mean that – although, to be honest, I was looking forward to – just us two.

JERRY. Sorry.

HORACE. No, you shouldn't be sorry.

JERRY. Anyway, the state she's in, it is just us two. So what did you mean?

HORACE. I don't know.

JERRY. What could I have told you?

HORACE. That you'd met her, that's what you could've told me.

JERRY. But I have told you.

HORACE. Like, you could've told me earlier. It's important. If she's important to you, then it's important. I need to know.

JERRY. It's only been going on for a week or so.

HORACE. She is important to you, isn't she?

JERRY. Yes, I suppose she is.

HORACE. I don't know what I'm saying.

JERRY. Anyway, you do know now.

HORACE. Yes. Right. I do know.

JERRY. They've got some mean dodgems.

HORACE. You're important to me, Jerry.

JERRY. Yeah, and you are to me.

HORACE. Like, I see our friendship as – special, not like any other friendship I've got.

JERRY. Yeah.

HORACE. And with you having done A-Levels early and pissing off to university –

JERRY. I might not've got the grades.

HORACE. Of course you'll get the grades. I'll miss you, and with another year at school and you not being there, I'll miss you, Jerry.

JERRY. We'll keep in touch.

HORACE. It won't be the same. That's what I want.

JERRY. There's vacations and things.

HORACE. Yes, I know, I know.

JERRY. And you'll make other friends.

HORACE. Well, I might do, but that doesn't change what I'm saying. I'm talking about you.

Beat.

It's going to be brilliant for you.

JERRY. Bollocks!

HORACE. It is, Jerry. You'll go right to the top.

JERRY. There's nothing stopping any of us from doing that.

HORACE. Believe me, you will.

JERRY. You'll go right to the top.

HORACE. Doing what?

JERRY. I don't know. Writing, that's it!

HORACE. I can't write.

JERRY. You can.

HORACE. Nothing special.

JERRY. You might. You could write a novel.

HORACE. A novel!

JERRY. Yes, that's it: write a novel.

HORACE. I'll never write a novel.

JERRY. Of course you will.

HORACE. What would I write a novel about?

JERRY. I don't know. Love, death, murder, passion –

HORACE. I don't have anyone to be passionate about, do I?

JERRY. That's no excuse. Beethoven wrote the Appassionata and he had no-one to be passionate about. Just imagine, Horry, in a few years time, we could both be doing our thing, and we'll bump into each other somewhere exciting, like we'll both be passing through Paris or Peking, and I'll have some gorgeous girl in tow – I know: Julie Christie! By then, I'll have Julie Christie on my arm.

HORACE. And who will I have on my arm?

JERRY. I don't know – Hayley Mills, and I'll say, 'Hi! How's things?' and you'll say, 'Fine. I've just finished my first novel,' and I'll say, 'Great! Send me a copy,' and when I get it, I'll think about us up here and how it all began.

JUDY snores.

She's worse than my dad.

HORACE. So you don't mind?

JERRY. What?

HORACE. What I've said about us.

JERRY. Why should I mind?

He takes a squashed Mars bar out of his pocket and unwraps it.

The munchies.

HORACE. Right.

JERRY. Courtesy of your local newsagent.

HORACE. Oh. Right.

JERRY bites the bar.

JERRY. I love Mars bars, don't you?

HORACE. I don't eat that much chocolate.

JERRY (*proffering the bar*). Give it a try.

He holds it while HORACE takes a mouthful.

What do you think?

HORACE. Mm. Quite nice. I sort of see what you mean.

JERRY has another bite.

Jerry?

JERRY. Mm?

HORACE. You know what you said about a bit of mutual?

JERRY. Yeah.

HORACE. You've done that, have you?

JERRY. Course. Haven't you?

HORACE. Sort of. There was this little kid next door in Edmonton. We used to do things in the shed. (*Re. the Mars.*) Do you think I could . . . ?

JERRY. Help yourself.

HORACE *has another bite.*

So – is that it?

HORACE. What?

JERRY. Things in the shed – that's all you've done?

HORACE. Kind of.

JERRY. Shit, Horace, all the more reason, mate. Go with a girl. It'll change your life.

HORACE (*coping with Mars in the mouth*). But I don't want to! You must know that! I want to do it . . . I want to do it with you. Sorry.

Beat.

JERRY. You'll meet loads of people.

HORACE. Yes, I might –

JERRY. Loads.

HORACE. But that wouldn't change – doesn't change – what I feel.

JERRY. There'll be someone clsc.

HORACE. No, I don't think there will.

They look at each other, face to face. Pause. For a second, they seem to get fractionally closer.

JUDY (*coming round, in a strong Birmingham accent*). Fucking beautiful!

HORACE *and* JERRY*'s moment is broken.*

I fucking love you, Jimi! (*Singing, still with an accent.*) 'After all the jacks are in their boxes . . . '

HORACE. Why's she talking like that?

JERRY. She does when she's just woken up.

JUDY (*singing*). 'The traffic lights, they turn on blue tomorrow . . . '

JERRY. Birmingham.

HORACE. Right.

JERRY. She's lost her accent, but it comes back when she's not thinking, like when we're doing it.

JUDY (*with the accent*). I love you, Jimi! And Brian, I love you, too!

JERRY. The first time, I thought I was bringing Beryl Reid to orgasm.

He steps into the room. HORACE *follows.*

Hey, Jude!

JUDY. Mm?

JERRY. How you doing?

JUDY (*without the accent*). Oh. Hi, babe.

JERRY. Hi.

JUDY. Have I been asleep?

JERRY. Yep.

JUDY. Oh, Christ!

She struggles to her feet. JERRY *puts what's left of the Mars bar on the floor and helps her.*

JERRY. Alright?

JUDY (*on the verge of vomiting*). Oh, fuck . . . .

HORACE. Hold on. It's only down the corridor.

JERRY. Hold on, babe!

HORACE hurriedly leads her out. JERRY lights a cigarette. He sits at the piano. He casually starts playing 'Pur Ti Miro' from Monteverdi's 'L'Incoronazione di Poppea', whistling quietly to himself. HORACE comes back in. After a while, JERRY stops playing.

Did she make it?

HORACE. Just.

JERRY. She's overdone it a bit.

HORACE. Yeah.

JERRY starts playing the opening of Beethoven's Fourth Piano Concerto with great aplomb. HORACE hovers, then gradually sidles closer to the piano ending up behind him. Pause. With great difficulty, he raises his hand intending to stroke JERRY's hair. Before he makes contact, JERRY breaks off playing. HORACE takes his hand away. JERRY stands. They look at each other. HORACE awkwardly removes his glasses. Beat. JERRY ruffles HORACE's hair affectionately and meanders over to the balcony. HORACE is left stranded. JERRY leans against the jamb of one of the balcony doors, holds his face up to the sun and closes his eyes.

JERRY. Mmm, Horry, feel that sun . . .

HORACE looks across at him.

(Sliding slowly down the jamb until he's sitting on the floor). Oh, yeah . . .

His back is against the jamb, his face still upturned and his eyes still closed. HORACE continues to watch. For a while, all that can be heard are the distant sounds of the fair. Then HORACE goes over to the dansette and takes off the record. Some pebbles land on the balcony unnoticed. As HORACE replaces the record in its sleeve, some more pebbles land, this time jolting JERRY from his reverie.

What the fuck . . . ?

BOY *(from down in the street).* Oi, poofter!

JERRY leaps to his feet and looks over the balcony railing as HORACE *dashes out.*

JERRY. Come up here and say that, you little sod!

HORACE. Ignore him.

BOY (*off*). I fucking will, mate, if you're not fucking careful.

JERRY. It'd make my fucking day, you little bastard.

HORACE. Oh, God, the neighbours! Keep it down, please!

BOY (*off*). Fuck you, shitface!

HORACE. Oh, Jesus!

Enter JUDY *looking the worse for wear, with streaked make-up etc.*

JUDY. What's going on?

She goes out on to the balcony.

JERRY. Some arsehole getting a bit lippy.

HORACE. Let's go back in.

JUDY. He's a kid.

JERRY. He's an arsehole.

BOY (*off*). Fucking lesbian!

JUDY. Cheeky little fucker! Fuck off, you little bastard!

HORACE. Oh, God! Please!

BOY (*off*). You fucking wait!

JERRY. We're waiting, arsewipe.

HORACE. Please! Look, he's going, okay? Let's leave it, alright?

JERRY. Little sod.

HORACE. We'll go back inside.

JUDY. No, hang on. I've had an idea.

She comes into the room and looks in her bag.

HORACE (*in the balcony doorway*). How are you feeling?

JUDY. A bit better, thanks.

HORACE. It helps sometimes, doesn't it?

JUDY. What?

HORACE. Throwing up.

JUDY. Oh, yeah, yeah. Don't really think about it.

She takes out a Brownie camera and goes back on to the balcony.

Right. (*To* HORACE). . . . Oh, fuck, what's your name?

JERRY. Horace.

JUDY. Fucking weird. Look, you stand next to Jerry.

HORACE does so. She looks through the camera.

Yeah. Move across a bit – get a bit of the view.

They do so.

Yeah. Great. Right, now, do something.

JERRY. What?

JUDY. I don't know.

JERRY puts his arm around HORACE's shoulders.

JERRY. How's that?

JUDY. Great! Now, smile!

JERRY and HORACE smile. She clicks the camera.

Fantastic! That'll be fantastic! (*To* HORACE.) You take me and Jerry.

She gives him the camera, goes to JERRY and embraces him. HORACE looks through the camera.

HORACE. If you move a little bit further apart –

They do so.

Very good. That's very good.

He tries to click it, but nothing happens.

HORACE. Let's have a look.

HORACE takes his hand and looks at the finger.

JERRY. It's nothing.

JUDY (*off. Singing*). 'Do you, don't you want me to love you . . . '

HORACE continues to hold his hand.

'I'm coming down fast but I'm miles above you . . . '

JERRY. It's gone all over you now.

He withdraws his hand and licks his finger again.

JUDY (*off*). Jerry!

Beat. JERRY *goes out.* HORACE *looks at the blood on his hand. He raises it to his mouth and licks it.*

JERRY (*from hall*). You coming, Horace?

HORACE. I'll join you later.

JERRY (*off*). Don't be long.

HORACE. The dodgems. Twenty minutes.

JERRY (*off*). See you.

JUDY (*off*). À bientôt.

The front door being closed. He looks at the chain, then goes to the mirror. He gently kisses it and puts it round his neck. Meanwhile, a pair of hands come into view, grasping the railings on the balcony. Then a BOY *pulls himself up so that his head and shoulders are visible through the railings. He checks the coast is clear and manages to haul himself up and over the railings. He's about 13 and has a fading black eye. The* BOY *spots him and creeps into the room, warily looking about him whilst taking something out of his pocket. He comes up behind* HORACE. *In a flash, he simultaneously pulls* HORACE's *head back by the hair and holds a knife against* HORACE's *throat.*

BOY (*sotto voce*). Where are your mates?

HORACE *is paralysed.*

(*Pressing the knife harder.*) Where the fuck are they?

HORACE. Gone.

BOY. Sure?

HORACE (*nodding*). Just now.

BOY. Where?

HORACE. The fair.

BOY. All by yourself, are you?

HORACE *nods.*

Little queer all by himself?

No response.

(*Yanking his head.*) Yeah?

HORACE *nods.*

You tell your mates that, if I ever see them, I'm going to cut their fucking throats out, cos I don't like fucking queers shouting at me. You got that?

HORACE *nods.*

(*Pressing the knife harder.*) I didn't hear.

HORACE. Yes.

BOY. Good.

He spots the discarded Mars bar. Keeping the knife at HORACE's throat, he reaches for it. HORACE takes advantage of this: he grabs the BOY's wrist and bends it back in an attempt to make him drop the knife.

Ow!

HORACE. Let go of it!

BOY. That fucking hurts!

HORACE. Go on! Let it go!

The BOY *lets the knife go.*

BOY (*rubbing his wrist*). There's no need to be like that.

HORACE *picks up the knife and examines it, as the* BOY *picks up the Mars bar and takes a bite.*

HORACE. It's rubber.

BOY. 'S'good, innit? Won it at the fair.

HORACE. What the fuck are you playing at?

BOY. Your mates pissed me off.

HORACE. You can't just come into people's homes.

BOY. I was like fucking Spiderman, straight up the drainpipe. Fucking amazing!

HORACE. And you shouldn't be climbing up buildings. It's dangerous. And anyway, what the hell are you doing being so unpleasant!

BOY. Unpleasant? I was fucking terrifying!

HORACE. No, you weren't.

BOY. I scared the shit out of you.

HORACE. Of course you didn't.

BOY. Course I did. Come on, own up, I was good, were'n' I? I saw one of my brothers do that to a darkie. He really did shit himself. Mind you, the knife was real.

HORACE. Look, fuck off, you little bastard, (*Re. the Mars.*) and that's not yours to eat, anyway! (*The* BOY *puts the last bit of Mars in his mouth.*)

BOY. He got Borstal for that.

HORACE. I'm pleased to hear it.

BOY. Second time round. He's fucking great. (*Looking round the room.*) Movin' out, are you?

HORACE. Moving in, and it's none of your business.

BOY. We live round here.

HORACE. Oh, Christ!

BOY. My name's Terence. What are you called?

HORACE. I'm not telling you.

TERENCE. I just thought, when we bump into each other –

HORACE. We won't.

TERENCE. Be like that! Anyway, we live in that new council
    block down the hill. You can see it from up-here. It's in a
    terrible fucking state already. The council don't give a toss.
    You smash a window and they don't do nothing about it. It
    freezes your bollocks off in winter.

HORACE. If you didn't smash the windows in the first place –

TERENCE. You getting smart?

HORACE. I think you should go.

TERENCE. Why?

HORACE. You shouldn't be here. I don't want you here. I
    don't like you, for Christ's sake!

TERENCE. Got any money?

HORACE. No.

TERENCE. Come on! My brothers have fucked off and left
    me. They've gone on the heath with the slag from the chip-
    shop and I ain't got a penny. Go on. Give us something.

HORACE. I said, no.

TERENCE. Tell you what, you can wank me for a quid.

HORACE. I beg your pardon?

TERENCE (*rubbing his crotch*). Go on, have a feel. It's nice.

HORACE. Absolutely not!

TERENCE. 'Absolutely', is it?

HORACE. I wouldn't pay for you if you were the last person
    on earth. Anyway, I don't need to pay for it, you cheeky
    bastard.

TERENCE. You should be so fucking choosy!

HORACE. Piss off!

TERENCE. Alright. If you give me that chain.

HORACE *instinctively raises his hand to his neck.*

HORACE. No.

TERENCE. I'll go if you do.

HORACE. You'll go anyway.

TERENCE (*snatching at it*). Come on, give it here.

HORACE. No!

He starts undoing it, backing off from TERENCE.

TERENCE (*stalking him*). Give it!

He snatches at it again, but HORACE *manages to pocket it.*

HORACE. Just piss off!

TERENCE *leaps at* HORACE. *They fall to the floor, scrapping,* TERENCE *trying to get the chain from* HORACE*'s pocket.*

TERENCE. I want that fucking chain!

HORACE. Get the fuck off!

HORACE *manages to scramble to his feet and move away.* TERENCE *leaps at him again and they crash into an upright chair. It collapses and they fall to the floor.*

Oh my God! They'll kill me! Aunty Pauline's antique chair! Look what you've done!

TERENCE. I didn't do nothing!

HORACE. Jesus Christ!

TERENCE *leaps on him again and manages to get his hand in his pocket.* HORACE *struggles to get him off.*

TERENCE. Where's it gone?

HORACE. Get off me!

TERENCE. It's not here.

He desists. HORACE *feels in his pocket.*

HORACE. You've nicked it.

TERENCE. I ain't.

HORACE. Give it back!

TERENCE. I ain't got it!

This time, HORACE *leaps on him, putting his hands around his neck.*

HORACE. Give it back!

TERENCE *starts choking.*

Give it me!

TERENCE (*struggling to speak*). I ain't got it!

HORACE *lets him go and starts crawling round the floor, desperately looking.*

(*Holding his neck, tearful.*) You could've killed me! I'll get my brothers round here, you wait!

HORACE. Please, please, tell me if you've got it! Please!

TERENCE. I ain't fucking got it! It must have dropped out.

HORACE. Jesus Christ!

TERENCE. It's only a fucking chain.

HORACE (*jumping to his feet and confronting* TERENCE). It is not just a fucking chain! Now, get out!

TERENCE. You wait, mate!

HORACE. Get out!

He grabs him and propels him through the door.

TERENCE (*off*). You ain't seen the back of me!

HORACE (*off*). Out!

A door slam. HORACE *re-enters and frantically resumes searching.*

It's got to be here, got be here . . . (*Looking everywhere.*)
Jesus, Jesus, Jesus . . .

The search becomes more frenzied. He ransacks the tea-chest, then starts moving furniture to look underneath, upturning various pieces.

It'll turn up . . . It's got to . . . It can't just disappear . . . Oh,
Christ! . . . It'll turn up . . . It will turn up . . . It's got to . . .

He starts to slow down and eventually stops, exhausted. The room is in chaos. He takes several deep breaths and finally calms himself. Pause. He closes the outside shutters, then shuts the balcony doors, darkening the room. He closes the door to the rest of the flat. He looks at the piano. Pause. Very slowly, he goes over to it and stands behind the stool. He raises his hand, then places it on the head of an imaginary person sitting on the stool. He gently strokes the 'hair', then bends to kiss the 'head'. He straightens up, his arms at his side, and stands motionless. 'Pur Ti Miro' from 'L'Incoronazione di Poppea' starts playing sung by two trebles with piano accompaniment. He closes his eyes. The lights fade and reach blackout as the music finishes.

End.